Let's Read About...
George Washington

For Keith, with all my love.
—K.W.

For Stephanie, with love.
—B.D.

The author and editors would like to thank Mary V. Thompson
of the Mount Vernon Ladies' Association for her expertise.

ISBN: 0-439-28135-0

Text copyright © 2002 by Kimberly Weinberger.
Illustrations copyright © 2002 by Bob Doucet.

Library of Congress Cataloging-in-Publication Data

Weinberger, Kimberly.
    Let's read about — George Washington / by Kimberly Weinberger.
      p.   cm. — (Scholastic first biographies)
    "Cartwheel Books."
    Summary: A simple biography of the first president of the United States.
    ISBN 0-439-28135-0 (pbk.)
    1. Washington, George, 1732-1799 — Juvenile literature. 2. Presidents — United
States — Biography — Juvenile literature. [1. Washington, George, 1732-1799.
2. Presidents.]
    I. Series.
    E312.66 .W44 2002
    973.4'1'092 — dc21
    [B]

2001034488

10 9

04 05 06

Printed in the U.S.A.
First printing, February 2002

Let's Read About...
George Washington

Scholastic
First Biographies

by Kimberly Weinberger

Illustrated by Bob Doucet

SCHOLASTIC INC.
New York   Toronto   London   Auckland   Sydney
Mexico City   New Delhi   Hong Kong   Buenos Aires

George Washington was born in
Virginia in 1732.
At that time, Virginia was one of
thirteen colonies.
The colonies belonged to the country
of England.

Young George grew up on a farm.
He loved to ride horses and catch fish.

George had many brothers and sisters.
He looked up to his older brother,
Lawrence.
Lawrence was a soldier.
He fought for England.
George also wanted to be a soldier
one day.

George did not go to school.
He was taught at home.
George practiced his handwriting
by copying rules of good
manners into a book.

At age sixteen, George went to live
with Lawrence.
Their farm was called Mount Vernon.
George rode horses and hunted foxes.
He danced at parties and practiced
his good manners.
He had never been happier.

At age 17, George had a very
important job.
He measured land using
special tools.
The land of America was still new.
People needed to know where the rivers,
forests, and mountains were.
George did his job very well.
He loved the land.

George grew into a tall, strong man.
In 1753, he became a soldier.

At that time, England and France were
fighting over America.
Both of these countries wanted to own
this new land.
George fought bravely for England.
In the end, England won.

Life as a soldier was very hard.
George was happy when it was time
to go home.

But he did not go back alone.
In 1759, George married Martha Custis.

Martha and her two children moved
to Mount Vernon.
George spent the next sixteen years
working as a farmer.

Then, in 1775, George was
called to war again.
This time, he would fight
against England.

The thirteen colonies of America
wanted to be free.
The people asked George Washington
to lead them in the war
against England.
George did not think he was
the right man for the job.
But he knew he had to try.

England was a very strong country.
The war went on for many years.
George and his soldiers were often
cold, tired, and hungry.

But they would not give up.
With George as their leader, the
colonies won their freedom in 1783.
They called themselves
the United States of America.

Americans now had to vote for a
person to lead their new country.
The choice was easy.
George Washington became the first
president on April 30, 1789.

George Washington was a peaceful
man who loved the land.
He had never wanted to be a leader.
But he served America both in war
and in peace.
As our first president, he is known as
the Father of Our Country.